W9-DHI-190

SHOW-ME
Bugs

Missouri Department of Conservation's mission is to protect and manage the fish, forest and wildlife resources of the state; to serve the public and facilitate their participation in resource management activities; and to provide opportunity for all citizens to use, enjoy and learn about fish, forest and wildlife resources.

There are many ways to support the Department's mission.
Visit www.missouriconservation.org to learn how you can help.

ISBN 1-887247-49-1

SHOW-ME Bugs

An uncommonly colorful guide to 50 cool bugs in Missouri

CONSERVATION DEPARTMENT · MISSOURI ™
Serving nature and you

by Michael Reinke | *illustrations by* Steve Buchanan

edited by Bonnie Chasteen | *designed by* Les Fortenberry | *technical review by* Dennis Figg

This book is for

THE CURIOUS AND BRAVE, BUG-LOVING PEOPLE OF MISSOURI

It will introduce you to some of the common and uncommonly strange bugs you're likely to find throughout the Show-Me state. It also features a few once-common species, reminding us to conserve habitat whenever possible.

PART ONE tells you what a bug is, as well as what it isn't. It compares insects and spiders in terms of their body parts (anatomy), and it discusses the way they develop (life cycle). Since bugs are among Missouri's most ecologically important wildlife, this section overviews the vital roles they play in nature. It also includes tips about collecting and studying insects and conserving their habitat.

PART TWO is a field guide. It groups related orders together and identifies the group's general body shape with an icon. Each species entry includes a full-color illustration, a few general details about the bug's appearance or behavior, where it lives and what it eats. The entry ends with an overview of the species' life cycle.

At the end of the book, you'll find a glossary of terms and a list of species organized by common name. Finally, a list of resources will help you learn more about insects, spiders and other creatures we generally call "bugs."

We hope you enjoy using **SHOW-ME BUGS** to explore the fascinating world of Missouri's insects, spiders and centipedes.

Contents

PART ONE: Show-Me Bugs

BUGS BY THE MILLION

Bugs are huge. Maybe not in size, but in volume they make up over half of Earth's species. By some estimates, about 10 million different kinds of bugs share the planet with us. If you knew their species names, it would take you a year to say them all. So far, though, scientists have found and named only 900,000 of the 10 million insect species they suspect exist. These 900,000 species make up 80 percent of all the organisms known to live on Earth. Here in North America we have an estimated 90,000 species of insects and spiders. They outnumber bird species by 100 to one. In terms of sheer numbers, bugs rule!

BUGS LIVE EVERYWHERE—EVEN ON YOU!

You can find bugs deep in caves, hundreds of feet under the water and all the way up to glaciers on snow-capped mountains. Bugs live in our houses and even on our bodies. One kind of tiny, squiggly, wormlike mite lives at the roots of our eyelashes! Every location in nature attracts and influences a particular kind of bug that is perfectly adapted to live there. In Missouri, you'll find insects that live on nothing but a certain kind of prairie plant, insects that thrive in clean streams, insects that inhabit swamps and insects that depend on mature hardwood forests. Of course, you'll also find insects that enjoy living with us, as well as on us!

THEY'VE BEEN AROUND FOREVER

Most bugs don't live long–only a few days to a couple of months. But insects as a group have been on Earth for a very long time. They appear in the fossil record 300 million years ago—even before the dinosaurs. They have survived global warming and ice ages several times over. In the process they have become diverse and widespread, and many continue to play critical roles in their environments.

BUGS RUN THE WORLD

Bugs are not only really plentiful and really widespread, they really matter. Without them, the world as we know it just wouldn't work. Without bees to pollinate plants, we would soon lose most of our food crops. And without fly maggots and other decomposers to do the icky work of breaking down dead things, Earth would soon be heaped with poop, garbage and dead animals. Although some bugs such as mosquitoes are definitely pests, other bugs such as dragonflies and fiery searchers help control pests. Next time you see a helpful bug, give it a salute. It's helping to keep Missouri green, clean and natural.

The fiery searcher eats destructive forest pests, helping to keep Missouri's forests healthy!

What's a bug?

"**B**ug" is a short, cute word for all the creatures in a big group (or phylum) called arthropods. This group includes insects, spiders and centipedes as well as shrimps, crabs and fossil trilobites. These creatures all have skeletons on the outsides of their bodies (exoskeletons) and legs separated into segments.

TRUE BUGS

Although most of us are in the habit of calling all arthropods "bugs," you will never hear an entomologist (a scientist who studies arthropods) call a spider, beetle, butterfly or bee a "bug." They reserve this term for the group of insects including stink bugs, assassin bugs and cicadas.

4

INSECTS (See diagram on Page 10)

Although insects and spiders are grouped together in the same phylum, they are very different. In fact, they are about as different from each other as humans are from mice. Humans and mice are both warm-blooded, have hair on their bodies and toes on their feet, but they are not close relatives. The same can be said of insects and spiders. Insects have three body parts: head, thorax and abdomen. The head has eyes, mouthparts and antennae. The thorax is where the legs and wings attach. The abdomen contains most of the guts. Insects also have three pairs of legs. Most—but not all—insects have one or two pairs of wings. They also have one pair of antennae that they use to smell the air for food, danger and other insects. Insects can be found feeding on many different things such as plants, other insects, larger animals and rotten stuff.

Although they don't look like it, centipedes and millipedes are closely related to insects. This is difficult to see because many of the features centipedes and millipedes share with insects are small or inside their bodies. However, you can see their antennae, which spiders do not have.

SPIDERS (See diagram on Page 11)

Unlike insects, spiders have only two body parts—the cephalothorax, where the eyes, teeth and legs are, and the abdomen, which holds the guts. Spiders also have four pairs of legs and no antennae. Almost all spiders are predators, which means they eat other animals.

So remember, when your mom says,
"DON'T TOUCH THAT BUG!"
you can say,
"ACTUALLY, MOM, THAT'S NOT A BUG—
THAT'S A CENTIPEDE ... THIS IS A BUG!"
Then show her a picture of a stink bug.

Insect

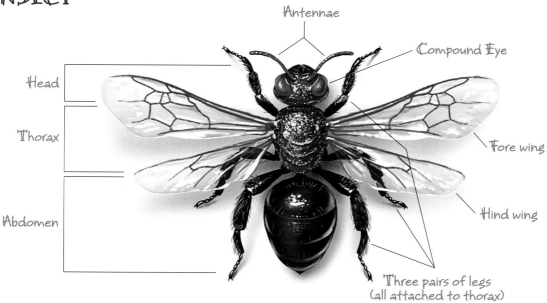

Antennae

Compound Eye

Head

Thorax

6

Abdomen

Fore wing

Hind wing

Three pairs of legs
(all attached to thorax)

Spider

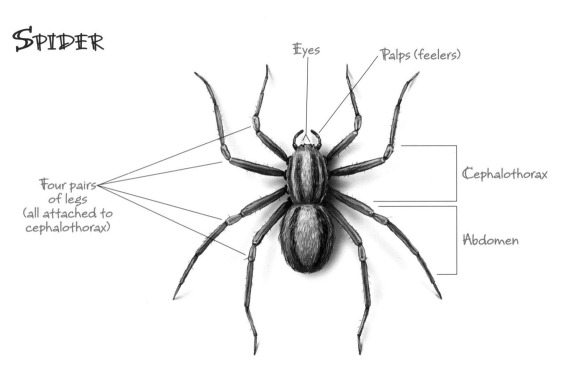

Eyes

Palps (feelers)

Cephalothorax

Abdomen

Four pairs
of legs
(all attached to
cephalothorax)

How they grow

An arthropod almost always begins as an egg, which the female lays. The egg hatches to reveal a soft-bodied hatchling, which quickly develops a hard, plated exoskeleton. The hatchling will shed this exoskeleton in a process called molting as much as 15 times until it becomes an adult. This striking change from egg to juvenile to adult is called metamorphosis.

INCOMPLETE METAMORPHOSIS

In this process, the young (called nymphs) look similar to the adult when they hatch. In most cases the nymphs live in the same habitat as the adults. They act similarly, eat the same food and are subject to the same dangers. Spiders, millipedes and centipedes—as well as some insects such as grasshoppers—go through this less advanced form of metamorphosis.

8

Eggs

Nymph

Adult

COMPLETE METAMORPHOSIS

In this more advanced process, the young (called larvae) look nothing like their parents. Often they are found in very different habitats, where they eat different things. When the larvae are almost ready to become adults, they form a pupa and go through their last changes inside this protective covering. The beetles, wasps and bees, flies and butterflies undergo complete metamorphosis.

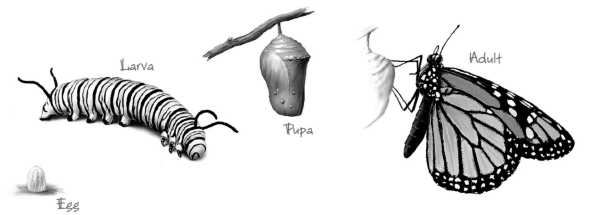

Larva

Pupa

Adult

Egg

How they look and act

Because so many different kinds of insects and spiders live in so many different kinds of habitats, they come in a mind-boggling variety of shapes, colors and textures. They also behave in dramatically different ways, depending on what they eat, what eats them and how they reproduce. The insects we see on a daily basis are brightly or boldly colored. This is because they want us to see them. They want us to believe that they are dangerous to eat or touch—and many are! We don't see the brown and green insects that mimic their habitats. They are trying to hide from other animals. Some (such as leafhoppers) are trying to not be eaten. Others (such as mantises) are trying to get close to other insects so they can eat them.

Arthropods can be organized according to what they eat. Predators make up a small but important group that eats other animals, such as other insects. The vast majority of insects, however, belong on the non-predator group. They feed on anything from plants to decaying plant and animal material to—in extreme cases—nothing at all.

Most insects eat alone, but some get together into groups for protection or to capture larger prey. Bees, ants and termites are famous for their social behavior. Some ant colonies can house millions of ants. Within the colony, certain ants spend their entire lives moving young ants and eggs around the colony, ensuring the success and survival of their group's young.

Color, shape and behavior are no accidents. They are special adaptations (species-level changes) that help arthropods thrive in their environments.

Most bugs are our friends

When many people think about bugs, the word "pest" comes to mind. Blood-sucking female mosquitoes, for example, are especially irritating.

In truth, the world as we know it would not exist without insects and their relatives. For example, we probably would not have flowering plants, which developed flowers to persuade insects to help the plants exchange pollen with each other. The insects were happy to help. If they hadn't been, we probably would not have apples or peaches or oranges, which depend on bees for pollination. Without insects, we wouldn't be wearing cotton blue jeans or silk dresses. Like fruit trees, the cotton plant needs insects to pollinate it, and silk is made from moth cocoons. Insects also feed many of the wildlife we enjoy (especially birds!), and some insects control others that are dangerous to humans. For example, dragonflies eat mosquitoes. Insects are even used in medical and scientific research.

Did you know that the wood roach plays an important role in the ecosystem? It helps return plant and animal nutrients to the soil, where they nourish new life.

Catch, study and release

You can learn a lot about the way bugs look and act just by watching them from a short distance. But because even big bugs have small features, you may need to catch and inspect them to learn more.

12   You don't need a lot of fancy equipment to collect insects. A net made with some fine mesh, a plastic jar with a lid (make sure it has holes) and a magnifying glass will get you started. Once you have the insect in the net, carefully coax it into the jar. After it is in the jar, put the lid on and look at it with the magnifying glass.

As you hunt and collect insects, remember that they are fragile animals. A butterfly or beetle can get caught in the net or die if you leave it in the jar too long. Be sure to return the insect to its habitat once you have finished looking at it.

NOPPADOL PAOTHONG

RULES FOR FIELD STUDY

Always go with a friend and make sure someone knows where you are going.

Some insects (such as the red velvet ant) sting.
Don't touch an insect unless you know what it is.

If you turn over a rock, put it back where you found it.

Stay off private property unless you have permission to be there.

The Missouri Department of Conservation has more than 900 public areas where you and your family or school can go to study and observe insects and other wildlife. Visit missouriconservation.org to learn more about your conservation areas.

13

Conservation

Insects and their relatives live in every part of the world. They were here on Earth long before the dinosaurs and they will be here long after humans are gone. One reason there are so many different kinds of insects living in so many different kinds of places is that they have adapted ways of taking advantage of every opportunity to eat and reproduce. They have done this in a manner that often helps their environment as much as it helps them. For example some insects sip nectar, pollinating plants and helping them reproduce in the process. Other insects protect their "host" plants from intruders or disease. Some insects prey upon other insects, keeping the prey population from growing too large and taking all the available food and space. Still other insects act as "decomposers" breaking down dead plants and animals and returning nutrients to the soil.

As you can see, the world needs insects just as much as insects need it. Because our survival depends on their survival, we must take care to preserve and protect them. The easiest and most effective way to do this is to protect their habitat—food, water, shelter and space.

Many insects can only live among certain kinds of plants and animals, and they can be very sensitive to changes in their habitat. In fact, if too much of a species' habitat changes too quickly, that species can become extinct (all its members die, and it ceases to exist).

This happened to the Xerces blue butterfly. It is the first butterfly in North America known to have become extinct because urban development consumed its habitat. It used to live on sand dunes in California where San Francisco currently sits. In the late 1800s, the city's rapid growth took over the butterfly's habitat.

Although you can still find the plants that the Xerces blue fed upon, there aren't enough left to support a population of them, so they are all gone.

Regrettably, this story is not an unusual one. Just one of our states, Hawaii, has the unfortunate distinction of losing 77 species of insects. The list will continue to grow until we learn how to better live in balance with the world around us.

Some insect species need large areas of a particular kind of habitat to survive. But you can help many kinds of insects simply by planting the native plant species they prefer. For example, the dazzling blue dogbane leaf beetle eats mostly dogbane, an easy-to-grow native plant.

16

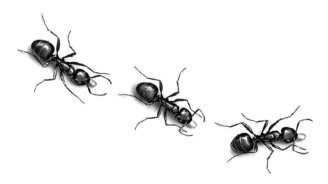

PART TWO:
50 Common Bugs in Missouri

Using the field guide

This section includes 49 species of insects and spiders you're likely to find in Missouri—plus one species that has disappeared from the state, but might be reintroduced in the future. The species are grouped according to order or family, the members of which generally have similar body shapes. These shapes are indicated by silhouettes (or icons). If the bug you've found resembles one of these icons, chances are you'll find a picture of it in this group of orders.

The species' common name tells you what ordinary people in Missouri generally call this bug. Sometimes a bug will have more than one common name, or two different kinds of insects may share the same common name. This is why scientific names are so important to scientists.

The scientific name includes the genus and species (although some entries in this book have the genus only). These scientific names are the same worldwide, and they allow scientists to discuss each species without confusing it with others. For example, both the giant water bug and the Eastern dobsonfly are commonly known as "toe biters." Their scientific names (*Lethocerus americanus* and *Corydalus cornutus*) assure scientists that they are discussing different species.

Spiders and
Centipedes

Mayflies,
Dragonflies and
Damselflies

Grasshoppers and
Their Relatives

True Bugs and
Their Relatives

Beetles

Habitat and food details are important because some insects can live only on certain plants or in certain places, and this information can help you identify the insect you've found.

Knowing an insect's life cycle can also help you identify it. Moths, for example, live much of their lives as caterpillars, which look nothing like the adults.

Size is another identifying feature, and the ruler will help you measure the insect you've found against others that look like it.

Perhaps the illustrations are the field guide's most useful feature. All are richly colored and finely detailed. Some include both the young and the adult versions of an insect, as well as some of its environment.

Nerve-winged Insects

Ants, Wasps and Bees

Moths and Their Relatives

Flies and Their Relatives

Black-and-Yellow Garden Spider

SPECIES:
Argiope aurantia

HABITAT AND FOOD:

LIFE CYCLE:

This spider is a common sight in flower gardens. Unfortunately, many people fear them, but they are harmless to humans. Spiders are not insects, but they are close relatives. The first body segment of the garden spider is covered with short, silver hair. The second body segment has a beautiful black and yellow pattern, which spreads across all eight legs.

Black-and-yellow garden spiders can be found east of the Rocky Mountains from southern Canada into Mexico. They are common in fields and meadows where their webs can be as much as 2 feet wide to catch the jumping and flying insects they eat.

The female garden spider is almost 1 1/2 inches long, twice the size of the male. She will lay her eggs in August or September in little, silky sacs she hangs from the web. The eggs hatch in the fall, but the young spiders do not leave the sac until spring. There is one generation a year.

The black-and-yellow garden spider's large, lacy web catches lots of insects.

| 0 | | | | 1 | | | | | 2 | | | | 3 | | | | 4 | | | | 5 | | | | 6 |

Daddy Longlegs or Harvestman

GENUS:
Leiobunum

HABITAT AND FOOD:

LIFE CYCLE:

Daddy longlegs are not true spiders. They do have eight legs, but they only have one body part, not two, as true spiders do. Daddy longlegs' bodies are only about 1/2 inch long, but their long, delicate legs can increase their overall length to 2 inches or more.

Daddy longlegs populations range throughout the United States. They can be found in grassy areas, but they are more common in wooded areas, under rocks or logs or inside caves. They will leave these dark areas at night to feed. Daddy longlegs have been known to eat anything and everything from aphids, to decaying plant matter to bird droppings.

Female daddy longlegs lay their eggs in the early autumn. The adults die during the winter. In the spring the eggs hatch and the young begin eating whatever they can find. There is only one generation per year.

Many people think daddy longlegs are dangerous, but they have no venom and their mouthparts are too small to bite people.

| 0 | | | | 1 | | | | 2 | | | | 3 | | | | 4 | | | | 5 | | | | 6 |

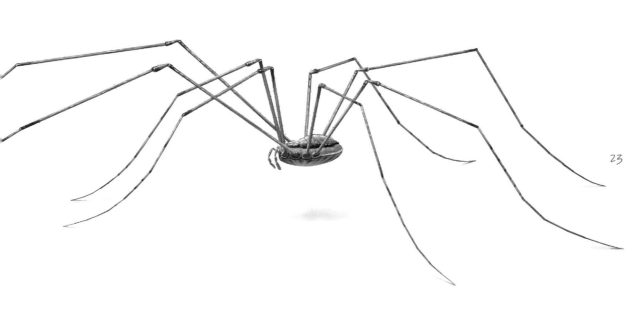

23

Giant Desert Centipede

SPECIES:
Scolopendra heros

HABITAT AND FOOD:

LIFE CYCLE:

At a whopping 8 inches long, the giant desert centipede is the largest centipede in North America. However, because it lives under rocks and wood, it isn't often seen. To ward off potential predators, it has a bright red head, a black body and a confrontational attitude.

The giant desert centipede is native to the southwestern United States, ranging from northern Mexico to southwestern Missouri. It is typically found under stones and logs on glades (rocky, desertlike areas) and rocky woodlands. The immature centipedes eat small insects, but the adults will eat any animal smaller than itself, including insects and small mammals.

The female lays eggs in hollow pieces of decayed wood. She protects the eggs until they hatch. The newly hatched juveniles have no color, but soon turn brown. As they grow, they develop the colors of the adult.

CAUTION! The centipede's CLAWS ARE SHARP and its BITE IS VERY PAINFUL.

| 0 | | | | 1 | | | | 2 | | | | 3 | | | | 4 | | | | 5 | | | | 6 |

25

7 | | | | 8

Biddies

GENUS:
Cordulegaster

HABITAT AND FOOD:

LIFE CYCLE:

Biddies are an uncommon kind of dragonfly. In fact, there are only eight species of them in the entire United States. About 3 inches long, biddies are brownish with yellow stripes on the sides of their bodies.

Biddies live in or near small, clear woodland streams. You can find them cruising slowly above the water. The nymphs eat small insects, tadpoles and worms. The adults eat flying insects. Generally biddies are difficult to find because their habitat is so limited.

The female will lay eggs one at a time inside wet wood or plant tissue next to a stream. After hatching, the nymphs burrow into the sand and silt on the stream bottom and wait for prey. When ready to become adults, biddies will crawl out of the water onto a stick and emerge. Adults can be found occasionally in the early and late summer.

Because Missouri has so many clean woodland streams, biddy populations are fairly good here.

| 0 | 1 | 2 | 3 | 4 | 5 | 6 |

27

Pond Damselfly

GENUS:
Enallagma

HABITAT AND FOOD:

LIFE CYCLE:

Because damselflies and dragonflies belong to the same order of insects, they can be difficult to tell apart. Damselflies tend to be smaller, and they hold their wings together over their backs when sitting. At rest, dragonflies hold their wings out at their sides. Damselflies belonging to the genus *Enallagma* are small, delicate, slow-flying creatures found near ponds and lakes.

Damselflies in the genus *Enallagma* live in and around ponds, lakes and wetlands. The nymphs live entirely in the water. Both the adults and nymphs feed on other insects. You can find damselflies throughout North America, but some species' ranges are shrinking as the clean water they need disappears.

Sometimes you can find adult damselflies stuck together. This is part of their mating ritual. Once mating is complete, the female crawls under water to lay eggs on underwater plants. There the eggs hatch and the nymphs develop. Once mature, the nymphs crawl out of the water onto plants, where the adults emerge. There is typically only one generation a year.

Males are blue with little black bands around their thorax, while the females tend to be gray.

| 0 | | | | 1 | | | | 2 | | | | 3 | | | | 4 | | | | 5 | | | | 6 |

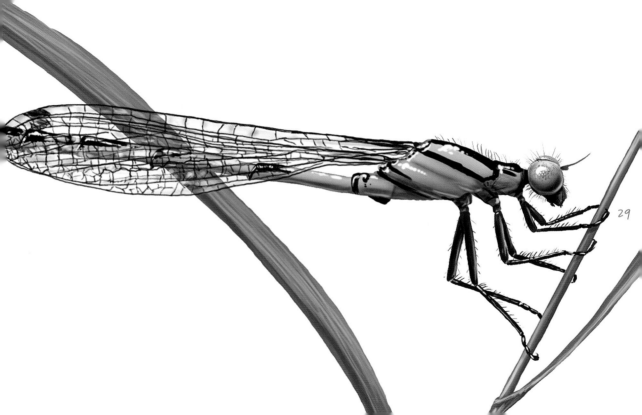
29

Stenonema Mayfly

SPECIES:
Stenonema femoratum

HABITAT AND FOOD:

LIFE CYCLE:

Mayflies are a fascinating group of insects. The nymphs live under water, breathing through gills on their abdomens. After a year of development, the nymphs float to the surface and emerge as adults. As adults, mayflies only live for a day or two, neither eating nor drinking because they have no mouths. The adults' only purpose is to mate and lay eggs before they die.

Stenonema mayflies live in fast-flowing creeks and small streams. The 1/2 inch nymphs snuggle under and between rocks, feeding on fine pieces of plant material. Some mayflies are extremely sensitive to water pollution, but the *Stenonema* mayfly lives in almost any stream that has relatively clean, fast-flowing water. Fly fishermen like mayflies because the adults emerge in huge swarms, triggering a feeding frenzy among trout and other insect-eating fish.

After swarming and mating, the *Stenonema* mayfly females lay their eggs in the water. The eggs drop to the bottom of the stream where they hatch and the nymphs develop. In April, all the nymphs in the stream float to the surface and become adults for the next swarm.

The nymphs are able to "stick" safely to rocks because their heads are shaped like shovels. This shape lets water flow over their bodies, pressing them against the rocks.

| 0 | | | | 1 | | | | 2 | | | | 3 | | | | 4 | | | | 5 | | | | 6 |

31

Chinese Mantis

SPECIES:
Tenodera aridifolia

HABITAT AND FOOD:

LIFE CYCLE:

Many people fear mantises but they don't hurt humans. The Chinese mantis is the largest mantid species found in Missouri. It can be up to 5 inches long, with mixtures of tan and pale green colors. This species was brought over from China in 1896 to help control crop pests. Many gardeners and farmers still buy mantis egg cases, each of which can yield hundreds of baby mantises.

You can find Chinese mantises sitting very still atop tall plants in meadows and gardens. They are waiting to reach out and grab any insect that flies or crawls by. To look for prey, they can turn their heads completely around without moving their bodies.

Eggs hatch in mid spring. The developing nymphs eat small insects. The adults appear in late summer. After mating, the females lay eggs in foamy masses, which they deposit on a twig or branch. Once dry, this mass looks like a nugget of hardened brown foam, and it protects the eggs until they hatch.

Many people call these insects "praying mantises" because their front legs resemble hands folded in prayer.

0 1 2 3 4 5 6

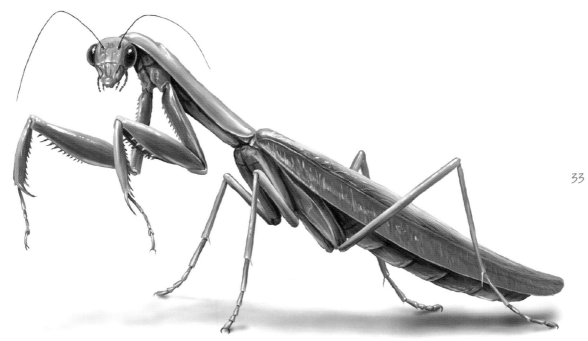

33

Common Walkingstick

SPECIES:
Diapheromera femorata

HABITAT AND FOOD:

LIFE CYCLE:

The common walkingstick looks so much like a tree twig that you may never see it hiding on a trunk or branch. When you do notice it, you may be alarmed by its size—up to 4 inches long—and strange appearance. Don't be afraid—the walkingstick doesn't bite and it eats nothing but leaves.

The walkingstick can be found in deciduous forests throughout the eastern United States. It eats the leaves of many kinds of trees and shrubs such as oak, redbud and cherry. Small numbers of feeding walkingsticks can stimulate the trees to grow new leaves. Too many walkingsticks, however, can eat all a tree's leaves, damaging it.

In the fall, adult female walkingsticks drop eggs on the ground under their host tree. In the spring the eggs hatch and the small walkingsticks climb up to start feeding on the leaves of the tree.

Hiding among twigs and branches, brown or green walking sticks are hard to see.

| 0 | | | | 1 | | | | 2 | | | 3 | | | 4 | | | | 5 | | | 6 |

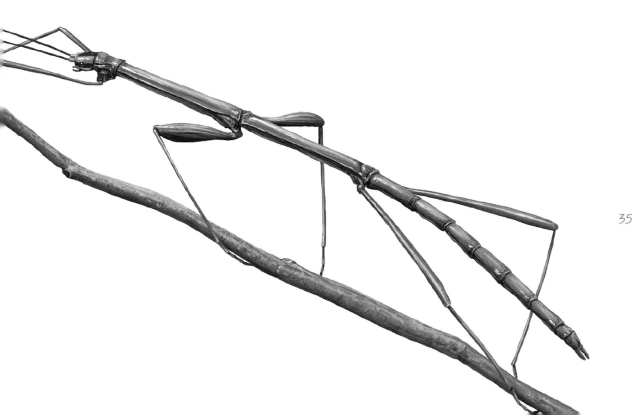

Differential Grasshopper

SPECIES:
Melanoplus differentialis

HABITAT AND FOOD:

LIFE CYCLE:

The differential grasshopper originally lived only in wet meadows and creek bottomland. With the spread of farms, however, it has become a pest of many food crops. The grasshopper population changes from year to year. One year you might see a couple in your garden; the next year you may see them everywhere.

Differential grasshoppers eat mixtures of grasses and other plants in crop borders, roadsides and gardens. They range throughout the Midwest, from the Mississippi River to the Rocky Mountains. When they run out of food in one area, the adults can travel up to 10 miles a day in search of more food.

Eggs hatch in late spring. The nymphs take just over a month to develop, and all of the nymphs become adults within a couple days of each other. The adults appear in early summer, and the females lay eggs in the soil from mid to late summer. They produce one generation a year.

Airplane pilots have reported seeing differential grasshoppers up to 1,400 feet in the air.

|0 | | | |1 | | | |2 | | | |3 | | | |4 | | | |5 | | | |6|

Eastern Subterranean Termite

SPECIES:
Reticulitermes flavipes

HABITAT AND FOOD:

LIFE CYCLE:

There are two different kinds of termites in Missouri. By far the more common one is the Eastern subterranean termite. A very destructive pest of buildings, eating the wood in and around homes, termites serve a good purpose in nature. They promote decay, which allows nutrients to return to the soil, where growing plants can use them. Almost any decaying log in the woods will have termites inside.

The Eastern subterranean termite can be found in every state east of the Rocky Mountains, where it is a destructive pest of homes. It eats dead wood, breaking it down into smaller pieces. Termites create colonies of more than one million individuals that can use an entire acre of land for their food area.

Termites have three castes—or groups that do different kinds of jobs—in the colony. The first group is the little white workers. Slightly larger soldiers have brown heads. A king and queen are responsible for creating all the eggs in the colony. They live deep inside the colony and are served and protected by the soldier and worker termites.

Termites may resemble ants; however, they are more closely related to grasshoppers and cockroaches.

|0| | | |1| | | |2| | | |3| | | |4| | | |5| | | |6|

European Earwig

SPECIES:
Forficula auricularia

HABITAT AND FOOD:

LIFE CYCLE:

European earwigs don't really creep into sleeping people's ears, but they do "hitch" rides with humans and their cargo. They arrived on the west coast from Europe in the early 1900s. The European earwig is about 1/2 inch long, with pincers on its rear end. The females have short, straight pincers, while the males have longer, curved ones.

European earwigs eat just about anything: other insects, ripe fruit, plants and even garbage. Because of this, they have become pests for many fruit growers. Earwigs can be hard to find because they come out only at night. They prefer living in garden plants, shrubs, woodpiles and under wood on the ground.

In the fall females lay shiny, white eggs in the ground. The males and females hibernate in nests with the eggs. In the spring females will protect the freshly hatched nymphs for a short time before leaving the nest. The immature earwigs become adults around September. The new adults then mate and enter the soil to make new nests.

BE CAREFUL! The earwig's pincers can give you a **PAINFUL PINCH!**

| 0 | | | | 1 | | | | 2 | | | | 3 | | | | 4 | | | | 5 | | | 6 |

Midwestern Salmonfly

SPECIES:
Pteronarcys pictetii

HABITAT AND FOOD:

LIFE CYCLE:

Like the mayfly, salmonflies are a favorite food of salmon and trout. As nymphs, salmonflies live in the water. The Midwestern salmonfly can reach over 2 inches in length.

In Missouri the Midwestern salmonfly is restricted to the Ozark regions of the state. Although the species ranges throughout the central United States, the Ozark population is completely separated from the others by farmland. Salmonflies live only in large, cold rivers or in cold water flowing over lake dams.

The adults lay eggs in the spring. The nymphs take an entire year or more to develop in the cold rivers. The adults emerge all at once in mid-April.

In mid-April, the adults emerge all at once, flying above the water in swarms, where they mate—if fish don't eat them first!

| 0 | | | 1 | | | | 2 | | | 3 | | | 4 | | | 5 | | | 6 |

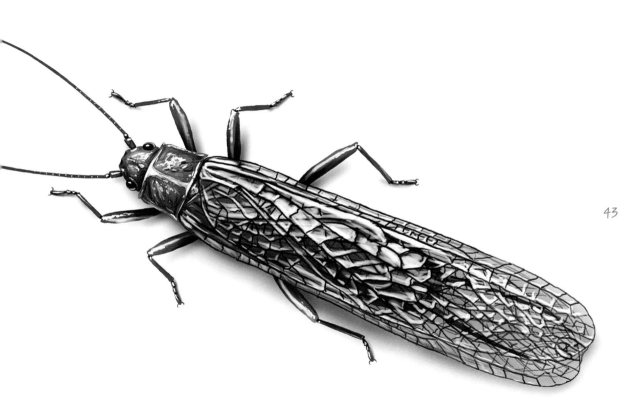

43

Pennsylvania Wood Roach

SPECIES:
*Parcoblatta
pennsylvanica*

**HABITAT
AND FOOD:**

LIFE CYCLE:

Cockroaches are much-hated kitchen pests, but most of our cockroach species don't come into houses. They prefer to live in the woods, far away from humans. One of the most common native roach species is the Pennsylvania wood roach. It has a shiny, dark brown body about 1 inch long. The females have little wing pads on their backs, but the males have fully developed wings and can fly well. Because they look so different, the two used to be considered separate species.

The Pennsylvania wood roach is very common, found in virtually every forested area east of the Rocky Mountains. Because it is a scavenger, preferring rotting materials including dead wood and insects, it likes dark, moist areas in open woodlands. You can find wood roaches in hollow trees, under loose bark or in piles of dead wood.

During the summer an adult female will lay an egg capsule containing about 30 eggs. These hatch a month later. The nymphs spend the winter hiding between pieces of loose bark. The following May or June they become adults and live until winter.

Roaches are "janitors" of the forest floor, cleaning up dead wood and insects.

|0 | | | |1 | | | |2 | | | |3 | | | |4 | | | |5 | | | |6 |

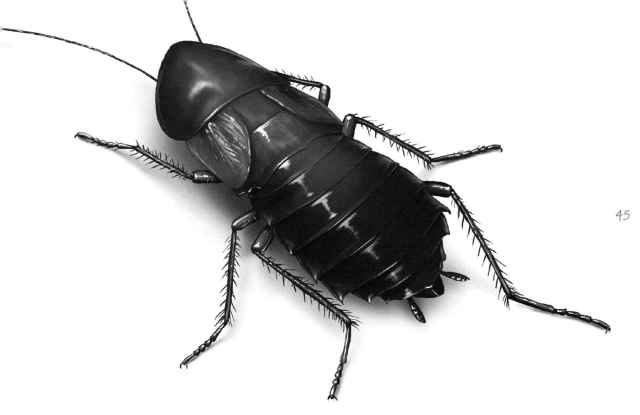

45

Prairie Mole Cricket

SPECIES:
Gryllotalpa major

HABITAT AND FOOD:

LIFE CYCLE:

When millions of acres of native tallgrass prairie covered the south-central region of our country, prairie mole crickets were common. Now that only 1 percent of prairies remain, the mole cricket is hard to find.

Because prairie mole crickets are limited to tallgrass prairies, most of their population is located on prairie remnants west of Missouri. They feed on the roots of tall grasses and animal matter from the safety of their underground tunnels.

Prairie mole crickets are hard to find, so little is known about their life cycle. They take at least two years to grow from egg to adult. The adults emerge between the first of April and mid-June. They locate each other by making chirping noises similar to those other crickets make. Their tunnels are trumpetlike, magnifying sound as it travels.

Like moles, prairie mole crickets live much of their lives under ground, digging tunnels with their strong, spade-shaped front feet.

|0 | | | |1 | | | |2 | | | |3 | | | |4 | | | |5 | | | |6 |

47

True Katydid

SPECIES:
Pterophylla camellifolia

HABITAT AND FOOD:

LIFE CYCLE:

The katydid is a master mimic. Not only does its bright green color match surrounding leaves, its wings are veined like them as well. Perhaps because they are so hard to see, katydids find each other by singing. They rub their front wings together to make a chirping noise, which they hear with ears located in their legs.

True katydids live mainly in forests and thickets, spending most of their time in leafy treetops. When they fall to the ground, they stumble around until they find a tree or shrub to climb. Katydids eat the leaves of most deciduous trees, but they prefer oak leaves. Because they depend on trees for food, katydids are spotty in large grassland areas.

One generation of true katydids occurs each year. Breeding begins in the late summer and early fall. The male will call in a female with his song. They mate and the female lays her eggs in the bark at the tops of trees. The eggs hatch in the spring and the young stay in the tree until they are fully grown, feeding on the leaves.

The katydid's shape, color and texture help it hide among tree leaves.

|0 | | | |1 | | | |2 | | | |3 | | | |4 | | | |5 | | | |6 |

Boxelder Bug

SPECIES:
Boisea trivittatus

HABITAT AND FOOD:

LIFE CYCLE:

50

In autumn you may see these bugs crawling on the outside of your house. They have mistaken it for a tree or rock, where they naturally prefer to spend the winter.

The boxelder bug gets its common name from its habit of sucking juices out of the boxelder tree. Surprisingly, this does not hurt the tree. Boxelder bugs also feed on other trees such as maple, apple and peach. Because of their limited food choices, boxelder bug populations can be spotty.

In the autumn large nymphs and adults congregate at overwintering sites, such as boxelder tree trunks. The adults come out at the end of March, and near the end of April they begin laying eggs in the crevices of boxelder tree bark.

Where you find one boxelder bug, you'll usually find hundreds more.

| 0 | | | 1 | | | | 2 | | | 3 | | | 4 | | | 5 | | | 6 |

Common Water Strider

SPECIES:
Gerris remigis

HABITAT AND FOOD:

LIFE CYCLE:

How do water striders walk on water? Their feet are like snowshoes, spreading out over the water's surface tension. The common water strider is typically about 1 inch long with legs extending about an inch wide.

The common water strider is a predator. It feeds on any living or dead insect it can find near the surface of the water. This includes mosquito larvae, other surface insects or insects that fall in the water from overhanging brush. They can be found on all types of water, from still ponds to quick streams and rivers.

Females and males communicate by sending water ripples to each other. Once they find each other, they mate and the females lay eggs next to the shore just under the water surface. Nymphs take about a month to become adults. They usually hibernate by crawling up plants or hiding under debris on the shore.

Water striders are fast because the little hairs on their feet allow them to push off the water's surface tension.

|0 | | | |1 | | | |2 | | | |3 | | | |4 | | | |5 | | | |6 |

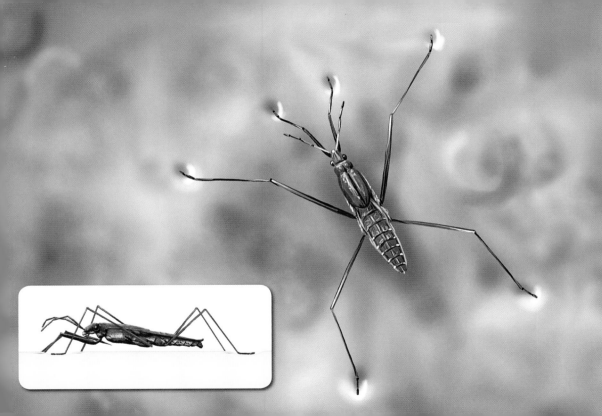

Giant Water Bug, Toe Biter

SPECIES:
Lethocerus americanus

HABITAT AND FOOD:

LIFE CYCLE:

Giant water bugs are big, often more than 2 inches long. They live in the water, eating other insects, tadpoles, salamanders and even small fish. They have also been known to bite people's toes, which is why they're also called "toe biters."

Giant water bugs can be found in ponds and slow-moving rivers throughout the Midwest, but they are much more common in the cooler waters of Minnesota and Wisconsin.

Late in spring male and female giant water bugs mate, and the females lay eggs on plants growing out of the water. For two weeks the males crawl up the plants and protect the eggs, keeping them moist by dripping water on them. The nymphs hatch and drop into the water where they live and feed on other animals until next spring.

Your toes may be happy to know that giant water bugs are fairly rare in Missouri.

0   1   2   3   4   5   6

Green Stink Bug

SPECIES:
Acrosternum hilare

HABITAT AND FOOD:

LIFE CYCLE:

Recognize this shield-shaped bug? You've probably seen it in your garden. It's called a stink bug because it gives off a bad smell when it's touched. This smell lets predators know that it tastes bad. Stink bugs are green or brown and measure from 1/2 inch to 3/4 inch long.

You can find green stink bugs in open meadows, field edges and flower gardens. They live by sucking the juices from the insides of plants, often creating big problems for gardeners and farmers.

Green stink bugs mate in the spring. They lay eggs in a honeycomb pattern on the undersides of leaves. About a week later, black nymphs hatch from the eggs. As they get older, red markings and yellow stripes appear on their backs. It takes about a month for a nymph to become an adult. The adult can live up to two months in the summer, but in the fall the adult will hide in the leaf litter on the ground and hibernate until spring.

Because they can feed on many different kinds of plants, green stink bugs are common and easy to find.

|0 | | | |1 | | | |2 | | | |3 | | | |4 | | | |5 | | | |6

Meadow Spittlebug

SPECIES:
Philaenus spumarius

HABITAT AND FOOD:

LIFE CYCLE:

Meadow spittlebug nymphs live in masses of froth on plant stems. This froth looks like spit, but it's actually a substance that protects the nymphs from predators. The adults are about 1/4 inch long with patterns of brown, black and gray on their wings and bodies. Sometimes known as froghoppers, they are among the best jumpers in the animal kingdom.

You can find the meadow spittlebug in any meadow or field. They feed on the juices of grasses and clover. Sometimes they can become problems for farmers who grow hay and wheat. The meadow spittlebug lives all over the United States and can even be found in Europe.

In the fall, spittlebugs lay their eggs in the inner, protected areas of grassy plants. The nymphs are small and yellowish, but they are usually hidden in the frothy spittle mass. They hatch in the spring and feed until June, when the adults leave the spittle mass. In August and September, the adults congregate on certain plants where they lay eggs for the following year.

Spittlebugs can jump almost 2 1/2 feet in the air. That is the same as you being able to jump over a 20-story building.

|0| | | |1| | | |2| | | |3| | | |4| | | |5| | | |6|

Periodical Cicada

GENUS:
Magicicada

HABITAT AND FOOD:

LIFE CYCLE:

60

The cicada's life cycle is a bit of a mystery. It takes years (13 or 17, depending on the species) for the insect to go from egg to adult. The nymphs spend all but one of these years underground, then the adults of the same generation all emerge together. How do cicada nymphs know when it is time to come out? Scientists are still trying to answer that question.

The periodical cicada is a plant feeder. The nymphs suck juices from plant roots, and the adults feed on trees and shrubs. Large numbers of adult cicadas emerging at the same time can damage trees and shrubs with their egg laying. Periodical cicadas live east of the Rocky Mountains.

In late June, adults cut little slits into tree branches and lay their eggs in them. Two months later the eggs hatch. The nymphs fall to the ground and burrow through the soil, feeding on plant roots for the next 13 or 17 years. In late spring, the nymphs come out of the ground and crawl up onto a tree or shrub. The nymph's skin splits, allowing the adult to emerge. The adults only live a couple of weeks.

In the summer it's common to find a cicada nymph's split shell clinging to a tree trunk.

| 0 | | | | 1 | | | | | 2 | | | | 3 | | | | 4 | | | | 5 | | | | 6 |

61

Potato Leafhopper

SPECIES:
Empoasca fabae

HABITAT AND FOOD:

LIFE CYCLE:

At less than 1/8 inch long, potato leafhoppers aren't very big. But they're everywhere, and they're serious pests for farmers. They suck the juices out of plants, stunting their growth. They can also spread plant diseases.

Both nymph and adult potato leafhoppers eat plants, and they are known to feed on more than 100 different kinds of plants. They can be found in just about every roadside, meadow and crop field.

The potato leafhopper is unable to survive the winters in Missouri. Every spring, a portion of the population around the Gulf of Mexico migrates up into the Midwest and Northeast. The adults lay eggs on the undersides of leaves, where nymphs emerge and suck the juices. In Missouri, the leafhopper will go through several generations throughout the summer until winter kills every leafhopper in the state.

Walk along a fence or a creek where the grass is tall. The tiny insects jumping all around your legs are leafhoppers.

0 | | | 1 | | | 2 | | | 3 | | | 4 | | | 5 | | | 6

63

Acorn Weevil

SPECIES:
Curculio glandium

HABITAT AND FOOD:

LIFE CYCLE:

The weevil family has more species (40,000) than any other family of living things on the planet. Many weevils have extremely long beaks with small mouthparts at the tip. Acorn weevils are no exception. The female weevil's beak can be as long its entire body. The male's is a little shorter.

The acorn weevil lives in oak forests, feeding on acorns. Unlike most forest insects that suffer greatly from deforestation, the acorn weevil can live in small stands of oaks, since thousands of acorns can be found on a single oak tree.

The adult female acorn weevil burrows into the center of an acorn, dropping in one or two eggs. The eggs hatch and the larvae feed on the inside of the acorn. In autumn, when the acorns fall from the tree, the mature larvae leave the acorns and dig about a foot into the ground. They spend the winter as pupae under the ground. The next summer they come out of the ground as adults.

Acorn weevils use their beaks to pierce acorns and eat them from the inside out.

|0 | | |1 | | | |2 | | | |3 | | | |4 | | | |5 | | | |6

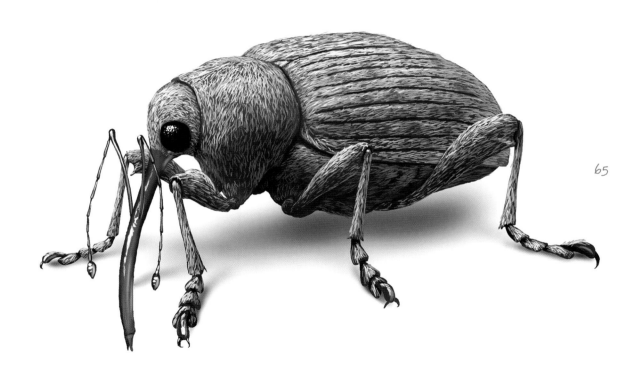

65

American Burying Beetle

SPECIES:
Nicrophorus americanus

HABITAT AND FOOD:

LIFE CYCLE:

The American burying beetle is a sad story in American conservation history. Before the spread of farms and cities, this bright orange-and-black beetle lived throughout the country east of the Rocky Mountains. Late in the 1920s, as farms and cities advanced, burying beetle populations began to decline. In 1989, the federal government put the American burying beetle on the endangered species list. Since then, efforts have been made to preserve habitats where the beetle can still be found and to reintroduce it where it has been wiped out.

The American burying beetle is a rare find indeed. Where they still exist, they prefer open meadows and grasslands as well as field edges. They are scavengers, using dead animals for food and reproduction.

Adults typically emerge late in the summer and feed until fall, when they bury themselves in the soil to survive the winter. In Missouri, they re-emerge in May and begin mating. The male and female both assist in burying the carcass of a mouse or other small animal. The female then lays eggs on the carcass. The larvae feed on the carcass until they mature, then they emerge to feed on other carcasses until winter.

The American burying beetle is no longer found in Missouri, but it may be reintroduced in the future.

0   1   2   3   4   5   6

Dogbane Leaf Beetle

A mixture of brilliant metallic greens, blues and bronzes, the dogbane leaf beetle can grow up to 1/2 inch long.

The dogbane leaf beetle lives in open fields, on roadsides and at field edges wherever milkweed and dogbane grow. Adults feed on the leaves, and larvae feed on the roots. Populations of this species are good, but it's hard to find large numbers of it in a single place.

Adults can be found as early as May in some locations, and populations build until late summer. Then the female lays small, yellow eggs in groups of two or three on the undersides of dogbane leaves. When the eggs hatch the new larvae drop to the ground and burrow down to the plant's roots to feed. The larvae will spend the winter underground. In the spring they pupate, then emerge from the soil as adults.

SPECIES:
Chrysochus auratus

HABITAT AND FOOD:

LIFE CYCLE:

The dogbane leaf beetle feeds on several members of the milkweed family, but it prefers dogbane above all others.

|0 | | | |1 | | | |2 | | | |3 | | | |4 | | | |5 | | | |6

69

Eyed Click Beetle

SPECIES:
Alaus oculatus

HABITAT AND FOOD:

LIFE CYCLE:

Most of the species in this family feed on the roots of small plants and trees, and some of the worst farm pests belong to this family. This species is different. The larvae can be found under tree bark feeding on immature wood-boring beetles.

The eyed click beetle can be found in hardwood forests where it is a predator of other beetles that eat hardwood trees. The larvae, known as wireworms, can also be found in the soil feeding on insects or roots of plants.

The female lays her eggs in the soil. Freshly emerged larvae enter decaying wood to begin feeding on other wood-eating beetle larvae. Mature larvae either return to the soil or find a protected site in wood to pupate. Adults are most commonly found around lights in the late spring and summer.

The eyed click beetle's big, white-rimmed eyespots are designed to scare away predators. Its actual eyes appear on its small head, which is hidden in the front of its thorax.

|0 | | | |1 | | | | |2 | | | |3 | | | |4 | | | |5 | | | |6 |

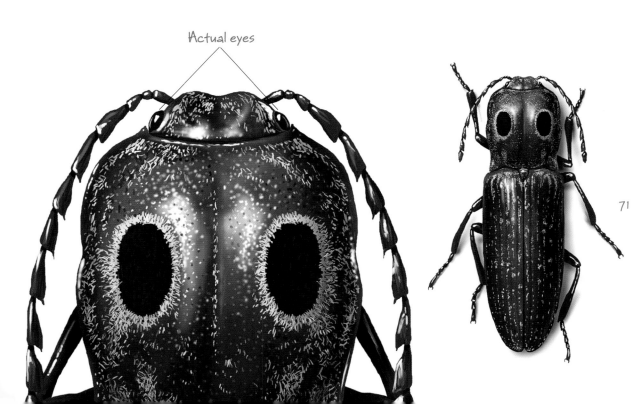

Actual eyes

71

Fiery Searcher, Caterpillar Killer

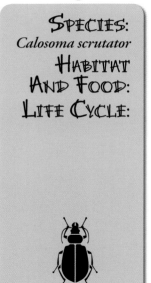

SPECIES:
Calosoma scrutator

HABITAT AND FOOD:

LIFE CYCLE:

The fiery searcher is very colorful, with a bluish thorax and bright metallic green elytra. You can find fiery searchers up in the trees eating or hiding under rocks, leaves or decaying wood.

The fiery searcher lives in open woods, fields and gardens. It gets its other common name, caterpillar killer, for good reason: it kills and eats caterpillars.

Fiery searchers are active from May through November. Adults can survive up to three years, hibernating in the soil during the winter. They lay their eggs in the soil, too. New larvae feed on caterpillars, then return to the soil to pupate.

Because the fiery searcher eats the caterpillars of such forest pests as gypsy moths and Eastern tent caterpillars, it helps keep forests healthy.

72

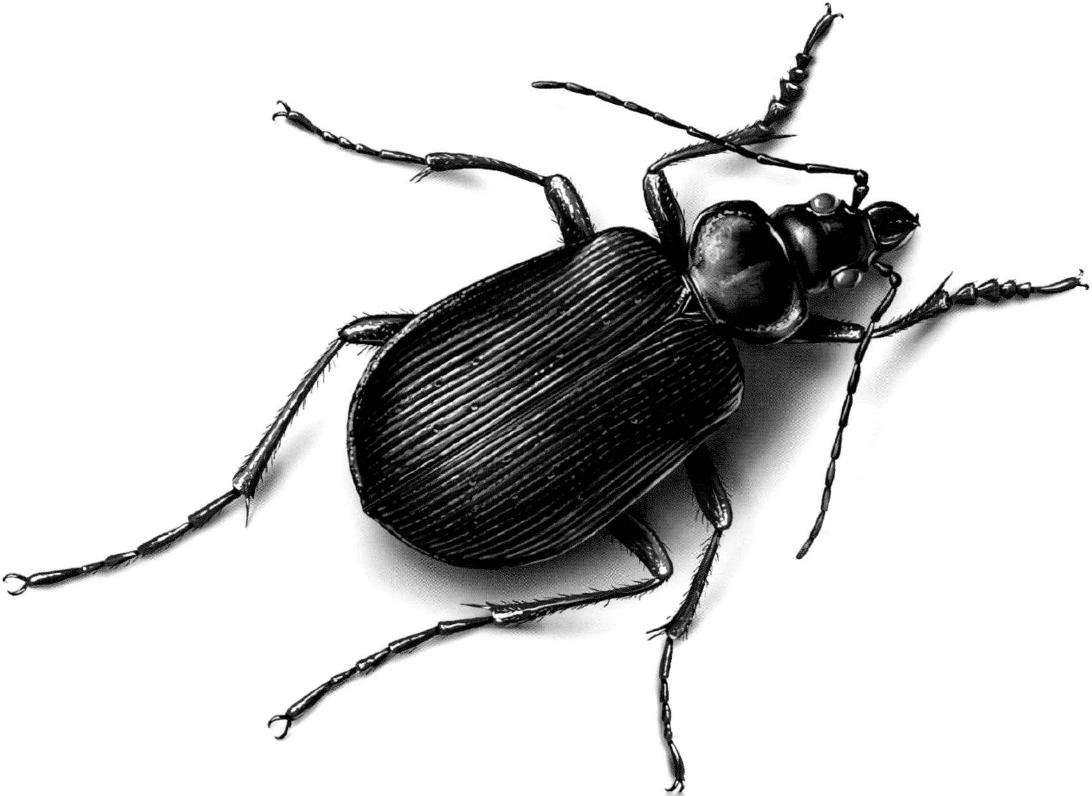

Eastern Hercules Beetle

SPECIES:
Dynastes tityus

HABITAT AND FOOD:

LIFE CYCLE:

The Hercules is the largest beetle in North America. The adults can grow over 2 inches long, while the young (grubs) can grow up to 4 1/2 inches long. Adults are usually olive-green or gray with dark brown or black spots. Males have two big horns that look like pincers. They use these when fighting for the chance to mate with a female. Females have no horns at all. Grubs look like pudgy, white caterpillars with three pairs of little orange legs.

Hercules beetles live in the East's mature hardwood forests. They feed on decaying plant material such as logs, stumps, leaves and rotten fruit. The adults eat tree sap and rotten fruit.

Female Hercules beetles lay eggs directly in piles of decaying wood. After about a month the eggs hatch, and the larvae feed on the decaying wood. The larvae grow for eight to ten months. Once a larva has reached its full size, it digs into the ground and hollows out a chamber in dead wood and debris. After a few weeks it hatches into an adult, but it stays underground until spring.

Missouri is on the western edge of the Hercules beetles' range, where numbers are few because they lack mature, undisturbed hardwood forests.

| 0 | | | | 1 | | | | 2 | | | | 3 | | | | 4 | | | | 5 | | | | 6 |

Red Milkweed Beetle

SPECIES:
Tetraopes tetraopthalmus

HABITAT AND FOOD:

LIFE CYCLE:

The few insects that can eat milkweed are foul-tasting and poisonous. The red milkweed beetle is no exception, and its red coloration warns birds and other would-be predators to stay away. One half inch long, the red milkweed beetle usually has antennae as long as or longer than its body.

Because milkweed is its only food source, the red milkweed beetle is limited to places where these plants occur—natural areas, uncut fields and roadsides. These places are great for maintaining milkweed populations, and therefore milkweed beetles.

Eggs are laid on the stems of milkweed at soil level in the fall. When they hatch, larvae feed on the roots of milkweed. Adults begin to emerge in midsummer.

The scientific name TETRAOPES means "four eyes." Look closely and you can see that this beetle has a second pair of eyes above the antennae.

| 0 | | | | 1 | | | | 2 | | | | 3 | | | | 4 | | | | 5 | | | | 6 |

Secondary pair of eyes

Primary eye

77

Seven-Spotted Lady Beetle

SPECIES:
Coccinella septempunctata

HABITAT AND FOOD:

LIFE CYCLE:

Ever wonder how the lady beetle got its name? In Europe during the Middle Ages, swarms of insects destroyed crops, and the farmers prayed to the Virgin Mary to stop them. Soon after their prayers, little red-and-black beetles arrived, eating the crop-destroying pests. The farmers called these "the beetles of Our Lady." Over time, the name became shortened to "lady beetle."

The seven-spotted lady beetle was introduced into the United States from Europe in the mid 1980's. Since then it has spread throughout most of the country. It feeds on small insects such as aphids. It has been so successful in its spread that the seven-spotted lady beetle has made other species of lady beetles harder to find.

The female lady beetle lays her eggs on the underside of a leaf near a bunch of insects for food. The larvae hatch and feed on small insects. The larvae go off to another part of the plant to go through their pupa stage. The adults can be found from late spring through mid-autumn.

The seven-spotted lady beetle has four black spots on each of its hard outer wings. When it rests, two of these spots overlap, making the lady beetle look like it has seven spots instead of eight.

0 | | | 1 | | | 2 | | | 3 | | | 4 | | | 5 | | | 6

Six-Spotted Tiger Beetle

SPECIES:
Cicindela sexguttata

HABITAT AND FOOD:

LIFE CYCLE:

The tiger beetle should probably be called the cheetah beetle. Like the cheetah, it's one of the quickest animals on Earth—moving up to 125 times its body length every second. It also has large eyes, giving it exceptional eyesight. Speed and sharp sight help the tiger beetle find and catch prey.

Habitat limitations make this beetle a challenge to find, but if you visit open, natural woods with clean creeks you might see a tiger beetle. It is a generalist predator, which means it will catch and eat any small insect or spider.

Adults appear in April and can be found through August. Eggs are typically laid around June and July. The female will lay them in a hole in the dirt and cover them up as if she were planting a seed. When the eggs hatch, the larvae burrow into the ground, creating a tunnel. To eat, a larva will sit at the tunnel entrance, watching for another insect to crawl by, then it will jump out and grab it.

About 1/2 inch long, the tiger beetle is metallic green or brown with white spots on the back.

|0 | | |1 | | |2 | | |3 | | |4 | | |5 | | |6|

Whirlygig Beetle

SPECIES:
Dineutus americanus

HABITAT AND FOOD:

LIFE CYCLE:

Groups of whirligig beetles swim in quick, random patterns, searching for food. Whirligig beetles have two pairs of eyes, one pair above the water surface and one pair below, to quickly and accurately find prey.

Whirligig beetles feed on other insects that happen to fall into the water. They are attracted to the waves insects make when they struggle on the surface. Whirligig beetles can be found in ponds, lakes and streams.

During summer, larvae appear in the water preying upon other insects. Whirligig beetles leave the water and crawl onto bordering plants to pupate. The adults return to the water. They overwinter as adults in surrounding mud and debris.

Although shaped a bit like bumper cars, whirligig beetles are able to avoid bumping into each other. They do this by feeling the waves caused by the others.

0 | | |1 | | | |2 | | |3 | | | |4 | | |5 | | | |6

Eastern Dobsonfly

SPECIES:
Corydalus cornutus

HABITAT AND FOOD:

LIFE CYCLE:

The male Eastern dobsonfly is a ferocious-looking beast. It's huge—often more than 3 1/2 inches long—and it has long, curved teeth that look like they could bite through steel. In fact, it's the female, with her smaller jaws, that can give you a painful bite.

Dobsonfly larvae, called hellgrammites, can be found in large streams and rivers. The larvae feed on other insects as well as small fish and amphibians. Like the adult female, the larvae can bite with their strong mouthparts. The adults are incapable of eating.

Female adult dobsonflies lay their eggs in large groups on branches or rocks next to streams. The egg masses resemble bird droppings to protect them from scavengers or predators. After hatching, the larvae crawl or fall into the water, where they spend the next two to three years. The full-grown larvae crawl out of the water to form a cocoon, where they spend the winter. The next spring, the adults emerge and mate. The adults live only a few days.

The male's long, curved mouthparts are used for courting, not biting.

0 | | | 1 | | | 2 | | | 3 | | | 4 | | | 5 | | | 6

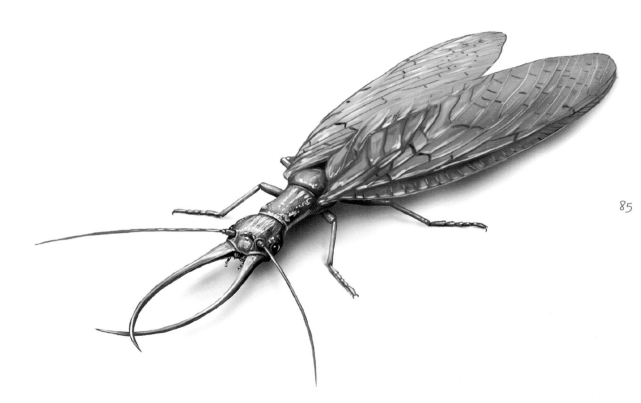

Green Lacewing

GENUS:
Chrysoperla

HABITAT AND FOOD:

LIFE CYCLE:

Although the adult green lacewing looks delicate, its larvae are juice-sucking predators. The larvae are brown or gray, flat and long, and have long, pinching mouthparts. Because green lacewing larvae eat many crop pests, farmers like to have large populations of them in their fields.

The green lacewing occurs throughout most of the country. It is rather common because the larvae feed on many different smaller insects. The adult, however, eats flower pollen and nectar.

The female lays one egg at a time. She makes a thin stiff thread, then she attaches one end to a leaf and the other end to the egg. This keeps the egg off the leaf and away from other predators. The eggs hatch within a week. The larva takes one to two months to turn into an adult. The adult can live for up to a month and a half. There can be several generations per year.

Adult green lacewings have long, thin antennae, little copper-colored eyes and clear wings with small, green veins.

0 | | | | |1 | | | | |2 | | | |3 | | | |4 | | | |5 | | | |6

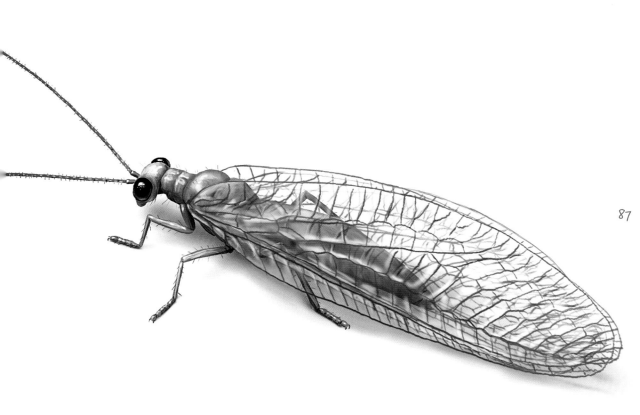

Black-and-Yellow Mud Dauber

SPECIES:
Sceliphron caementarium

HABITAT AND FOOD:

LIFE CYCLE:

The black-and-yellow mud dauber is a cousin to the paper wasp. They both make nests, but the mud dauber uses mud instead of chewed wood. Female mud daubers gather mud and build many-celled nests under rock faces or overhangs. You will find only one mud dauber on each nest, but several females will make nests near each other.

Black-and-yellow mud dauber populations are found all over the country. They are common in meadows and back yards with wet ground and suitable nesting sites. The adults feed on nectar from flowers, but the young feed on spiders. The adult female will capture and kill spiders, then place them in cells with an egg. When the egg hatches, the larva feeds on the spiders until it emerges as an adult.

Adults can be found from June through most of September. Eggs hatch late in the summer and feed on the spiders that have been sealed inside their mud cells. The larvae pupate in the fall, but remain in the mud nest until early the next summer when they emerge as adults.

These black-and-yellow wasps avoid stinging people, reserving their venom to kill prey. STILL, THEY CAN HURT YOU IF YOU PICK THEM UP.

|0 | | | |1 | | | |2 | | | |3 | | | |4 | | | |5 | | | |6|

Carpenter Ant

SPECIES:
Camponotus pennsylvanicus

HABITAT AND FOOD:

LIFE CYCLE:

A carpenter ant colony is a great example of social organization in the insect world. Mature colonies can consist of several thousand individuals performing many different jobs, such as gathering food, protecting the colony and taking care of the young. At less than half an inch long, ants can pack into tight places such as decaying logs, dead trees and between walls in houses.

Carpenter ants build their colonies in damp wood, hollowing out chambers as the colony gets bigger. They do not eat the wood. They make little piles of the removed wood as well as scraps of trash outside the colony. They like to eat other insects, plant juices and honeydew from aphids, and they will also help themselves to your picnic scraps.

Ants start coming out of colonies to look for food on the first warm spring days. They are active throughout the day, every day, by May. Mature colonies begin producing winged ants in the spring and release them from May through June. These winged ants mate and produce a new colony. Each colony begins with one queen who produces all the eggs.

A single ant colony has the capability of living up to 10 years or more.

0 | | |1 | | | |2 | | |3 | | |4 | | |5 | | |6

Carpenter Bee

SPECIES:
Xylocopa virginica

HABITAT AND FOOD:

LIFE CYCLE:

Many people complain about "bumblebees" flying around under their gutters. In fact, these are carpenter bees looking for places to build their nests. You can also find carpenter bees in gardens and fields, flying from flower to flower, looking for nectar and pollen. The back of the carpenter bee's abdomen is shiny black because it has very few hairs, while the bumblebee's abdomen is covered in black and yellow hairs.

Carpenter bees burrow nest holes in dead wood. They especially like pine trees. Later generations will use old burrows, so a nest can be a problem for years. They do not like wood treated with varnish or paint. Carpenter bees do not eat the wood; they feed upon plant nectar and pollen.

Typically carpenter bees have only one generation a year. They overwinter as adults, then mate in the spring. The female will lay 6-8 eggs, one at a time. Each egg gets its own chamber with a small amount of food. The new adults show up late in the summer.

Although they look threatening, male carpenter bees lack stingers, and the females are reluctant to sting.

| 0 | | | 1 | | | 2 | | | 3 | | | 4 | | | 5 | | | 6 |

Cross section
of carpenter
bee nest.
Illustration
not drawn to
scale with bee
at right.

93

European Hornet

SPECIES:
Vespa crabro

HABITAT AND FOOD:

LIFE CYCLE:

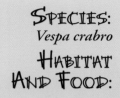

The European hornet arrived in New York from Europe in the mid-1800s, but it took another 100 years for it to appear in Missouri. The European hornet is mild-mannered, attacking only when it or its nest is threatened.

The European hornet can be found throughout the eastern United States. Missouri and Arkansas are on the western edge of the hornet's range, but it is spreading west. European hornets prefer wooded environments but have been known to make nests in home attics. They feed on other insects and attack honeybee hives, eating adult bees and their larvae.

European hornets make nests out of chewed-up wood pulp, usually in low buildings or hollow trees. The female makes a new nest each spring and lays her eggs in it. As workers emerge, they take over nest-keeping duties. A mature nest can have as many as 1,000 workers. The colony remains active until mid October.

You can tell European hornets from other hornets by their color pattern and large size (up to 1 1/2 inches long). Be careful observing the European hornet BECAUSE THE STING IS VERY PAINFUL.

| 0 | | | 1 | | | | 2 | | | 3 | | | 4 | | | 5 | | | 6 |

95

Giant Ichneumon

SPECIES:
Megarhyssa atrata

HABITAT AND FOOD:

LIFE CYCLE:

The giant ichneumon (ick-NEW-mon) is a rare find in Missouri, which has little suitable habitat for it. Including its long, thin "tail," the ichneumon is more than 6 inches long. Although it looks dangerous, the ichneumon is harmful only to the larvae of other wasps, which ichneumon larvae eat.

The giant ichneumon can be found in large tracts of old, deciduous forests throughout the eastern United States. Missouri, with few old forests, is at the western limit of its range. Ichneumon larvae feed upon larvae of the pigeon horntail, another kind of wasp that lays its eggs in dead wood.

Giant ichneumons appear May through July. The female locates pigeon horntail larvae in dead wood then weaves her long egg tube into the nest, depositing an egg. When the egg hatches, the larva feeds on the pigeon horntail larvae.

The ichneumon's long, whiplike tail is actually a soft, flexible tube. Females weave it into logs or trees, then deposit eggs on the larvae of horntail wasps living there.

Paper Wasp

SPECIES:
Polistes metricus

HABITAT
AND FOOD:

LIFE CYCLE:

98

There isn't an old barn in Missouri that doesn't host a colony of paper wasps. To make its large, balloon-shaped nest, the female scrapes wood fibers from old boards and dry wood. It chews the fibers, mixing them with its saliva, and creating a thin paper, which it forms into open cells hung from a single stalk.

As Missouri became settled, paper wasp populations increased, and now they are all over the state. This is because people provide protected areas such as houses, barns and buildings for their nests. With their painful stings, paper wasps can be a nuisance, but they also help people by getting rid of garden pests. Adults feed on nectar, but they collect caterpillars to use as food for their larvae.

In the spring a female that mated the previous fall begins a nest on her own. Her first generation of eggs will all hatch as females. These grow up to become workers, collecting food and paper to serve the nest. If the dominant female gets killed, another female will begin to lay eggs, but these new eggs make male adults.

FEMALE PAPER WASPS CAN DELIVER A
PAINFUL STING, so don't get too close.

0   1   2   3   4   5   6

Red Velvet Ant, Cow Killer

SPECIES:
Dasymutilla occidentalis

HABITAT AND FOOD:

LIFE CYCLE:

Velvet ants are related to ants, but they are actually wasps. They live alone, not in social groups as ants do. Female velvet ants, which do not have wings, crawl on the ground, searching for nectar and bumblebee nests in which to lay their eggs. The males are a little smaller, but they have wings and fly over the ground looking for females to mate with.

You can find velvet ants in old fields, meadows and forest edges throughout the Midwest. Both males and females get their energy from eating nectar. Velvet ants don't gather in large populations, but if you find one, more are probably nearby.

Red velvet ants are parasites of bumblebees. A female velvet ant will dig into a bumblebee nest, find a larva and lay an egg in it. When the egg hatches, the velvet ant larva will feed on the bumblebee larva. Adult velvet ants can be found throughout the warm summer months.

The red velvet ant is pretty, but don't touch it! ITS STING IS SO PAINFUL THAT SOME PEOPLE CALL IT "COW KILLER."

0 | | | 1 | | | 2 | | | 3 | | | 4 | | | 5 | | | 6

Caddisfly

Adult caddisflies look like small, brown moths with extra long antennae. The larvae, however, live under water where they make special shells to live in until it is time for them to crawl to the surface and become adults.

Helicopsyche (hee-lee-koh-SIGH-kee) caddisfly larvae can be found in fast-moving streams all over the country. To eat, they use their strong jaws to scrape plant material off rocks. They can withstand wide ranges in water temperature, from hot springs to cold mountain streams.

In the summer adults lay their eggs in the water, but the eggs don't hatch until the late fall. The larvae hide among the rocks, making protective cases from small grains of sand, which they bind together with silk.

SPECIES:
Helicopsyche borealis

HABITAT AND FOOD:

LIFE CYCLE:

HELICOPSYCHE caddisfly larvae build cases that look like snail shells, which they live in until they become adults.

| 0 | | | |1 | | | |2 | | | |3 | | | |4 | | | |5 | | | |6 |

Hickory Horned Devil

SPECIES:
Citheronia regalis

HABITAT AND FOOD:

LIFE CYCLE:

The hickory horned devil (known as the regal moth or royal walnut moth) is among the largest, most colorful moths in the country. The caterpillars, however, win the prize for size and scariness. They can be almost 6 inches long, with huge, inch-long, black-and-orange spines on the backs of their heads.

The caterpillar feeds on many kinds of native nut trees, such as hickory and walnut, and it will eat ash and sycamore as well. The adults do not eat, living only to mate and lay eggs to start the next generation. Both caterpillar and adult are found in healthy, mature forests throughout the eastern half of the country. With its few large tracts of mature forest, Missouri lies at the western edge of the hickory horned devil's range.

The adults appear from June through July. They fly at night, searching for mates. After mating, the females lay their eggs in trees. The eggs take about a week to hatch, then the caterpillars spend the next month and a half eating as much as they can. Late in the summer the caterpillars crawl out of the trees and bury themselves in the ground to pupate until the next summer. In Missouri only one generation is produced per year.

If you reach for it, the caterpillar will lift its head and swing its spines at you. Not to worry, though; it is harmless.

| 0 | | | | 1 | | | | 2 | | | 3 | | | 4 | | | 5 | | | 6 |

The adult hickory horned devil is known as the regal moth

105

Caterpillar

Luna Moth

SPECIES:
Actias luna

HABITAT AND FOOD:

LIFE CYCLE:

At 4 to 5 inches wide, luna moths are bigger than some birds and bats. All four of their pale green wings have eyespots. These may convince predators that the luna is a whole group of animals instead of a single moth. Lunas use their large, antler-like antennae to "smell" for other luna moths. Active at night, they are attracted to lights, such as the moon, from which they get their name.

The luna moth can be found in hardwood forests. The larvae eat walnut, hickory and persimmon leaves. The adults have no mouths and do not feed. They live only to mate, lay eggs, then die in about a week.

The adults lay eggs on the undersides of native nut and persimmon leaves, and the caterpillars feed on them when they hatch. The green caterpillars grow up to 3 1/2 inches long before gathering plant material to make a cocoon. Missouri gets two generations of luna moths a year. The first generation of adults comes out of cocoons in late April. The second generation comes out in late July or August.

Because they depend on forests, luna moth populations shrink when forests are cut.

|0 | | | |1 | | | |2 | | | |3 | | | |4 | | | |5 | | | |6|

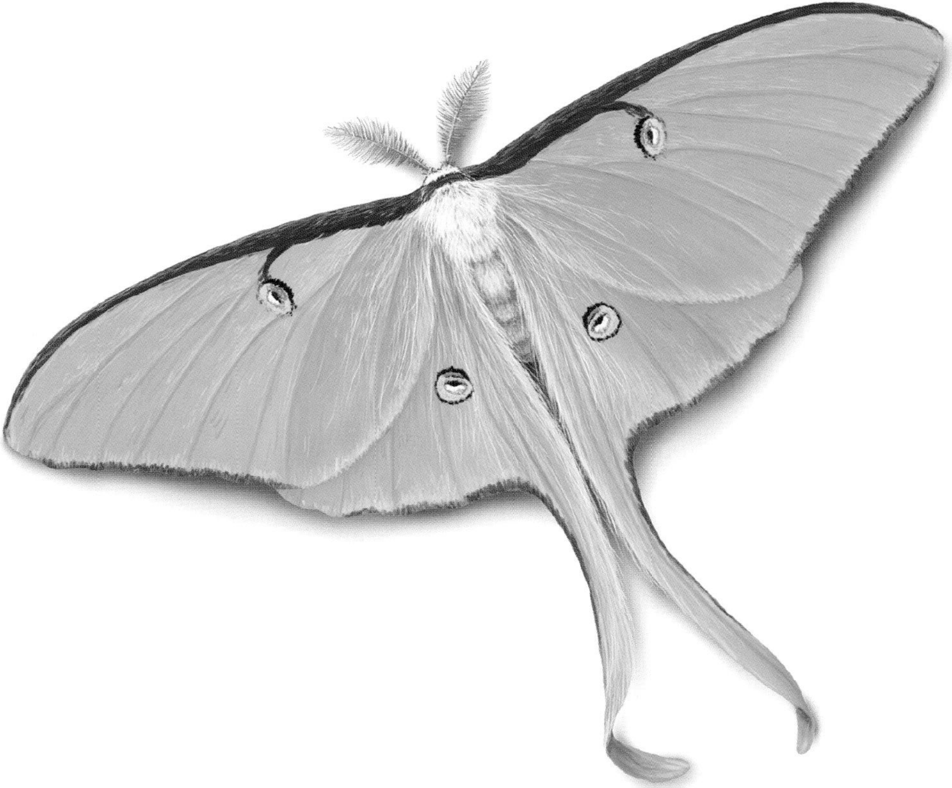

Woolly Bear Caterpillar

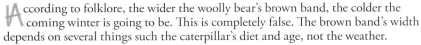

SPECIES:
Pyrrharctia isabella

HABITAT AND FOOD:

LIFE CYCLE:

According to folklore, the wider the woolly bear's brown band, the colder the coming winter is going to be. This is completely false. The brown band's width depends on several things such the caterpillar's diet and age, not the weather.

The banded woolly bear is common in fields and road edges. It feeds on small, green plants such as dandelions. In the fall, you will see it crossing roads in search of a good hibernation site.

The banded woolly bear can be found in large numbers in the fall and the spring. This is the same generation. It overwinters as a mature caterpillar, and then uses its bristly hairs to make its cocoon in the spring. The adult moths can be found April through September. There can be one or two generations a year.

Woolly bears are fun to pick up and examine, but THEIR BRISTLY HAIRS MAY IRRITATE SENSITIVE SKIN.

| 0 | | | | 1 | | | | 2 | | | | 3 | | | | 4 | | | | 5 | | | | 6 |

109

Adult wolly bears
are known as
Isabella tiger moths

Asian Tiger Mosquito

SPECIES:
Aedes albopictus

HABITAT AND FOOD:

LIFE CYCLE:

The Asian tiger mosquito arrived from Asia in shipments of old tires in 1985. In other parts of the world, this species transmits several deadly diseases, most of which do not occur in the United States. The Asian tiger mosquito is about 1/4 inch long. It is black with white bands on its legs and mouth, and a white stripe down its head and thorax.

They are native to Southeast Asia but have spread throughout most of the world, including the eastern and southern United States. The larvae are found in standing water, and the adults are never far away. The females drink blood from humans as well as other animals and birds.

Adult Asian tiger mosquitoes lay their eggs above containers of water, such as flowerpots, birdbaths or gutters. The eggs hatch and the larvae drop into the water, developing and becoming adults in two weeks. There are several generations a year.

Only female mosquitoes suck blood, which they need in order to develop eggs. Males feed on nectar and plant juices.

|0 | | |1 | | |2 | | |3 | | |4 | | |5 | | |6

Black Horse Fly

SPECIES:
Tabanus atratus

HABITAT AND FOOD:

LIFE CYCLE:

There are several species of horse flies in Missouri, but the most recognizable is the black horse fly. It is large, with a bluish-black body and black wings that can reach over an inch in length.

Most Missouri horse fly larvae are aquatic. They can be found in mud in ponds and streams, and the adults live in the vicinity of permanent water sources. Only the females bite people and animals. They do this because they, like female mosquitoes, need the raw materials found in blood to produce eggs.

The adult female lays eggs on vegetation near ponds and streams. The eggs hatch and the larvae drop into the water and mud where they live up to several years. Once ready, the larvae leave the water to pupate. All individuals of a horse fly species become adults at the same time. This makes it easier for the males to find the females.

Common horse flies are regular pests on farms, where they swarm and bite cattle, horses and other animals.

| 0 | | | | 1 | | | | 2 | | | | 3 | | | | 4 | | | | 5 | | | | 6 |

Crane Fly

Many people are frightened of crane flies, which look like huge mosquitoes. But crane flies don't bite or suck blood. In fact, they don't have mouths at all. There are many species of crane flies, and they can be found all over the country in almost any habitat. Because the larvae of many crane fly species can live only in clean water, scientists can use them to tell how clean a stream is.

GENUS:
Tipula

HABITAT AND FOOD:

Crane flies can be found throughout the country. Most are limited to moist habitats such as woods, grassy meadows and stream edges. The larvae are almost always found in streams and lakes feeding on leaf debris.

LIFE CYCLE:

Different species of crane flies can be found throughout the spring, summer and fall. The adult females lay their eggs either under water or in soil next to water. The larvae develop under water. Most crane flies have only one generation a year.

Some crane flies can be up to 1 1/2 inches long. The adults eat nothing, living only to mate and lay eggs.

|0 | | | |1 | | | | |2 | | | |3 | | | |4 | | | |5 | | | |6

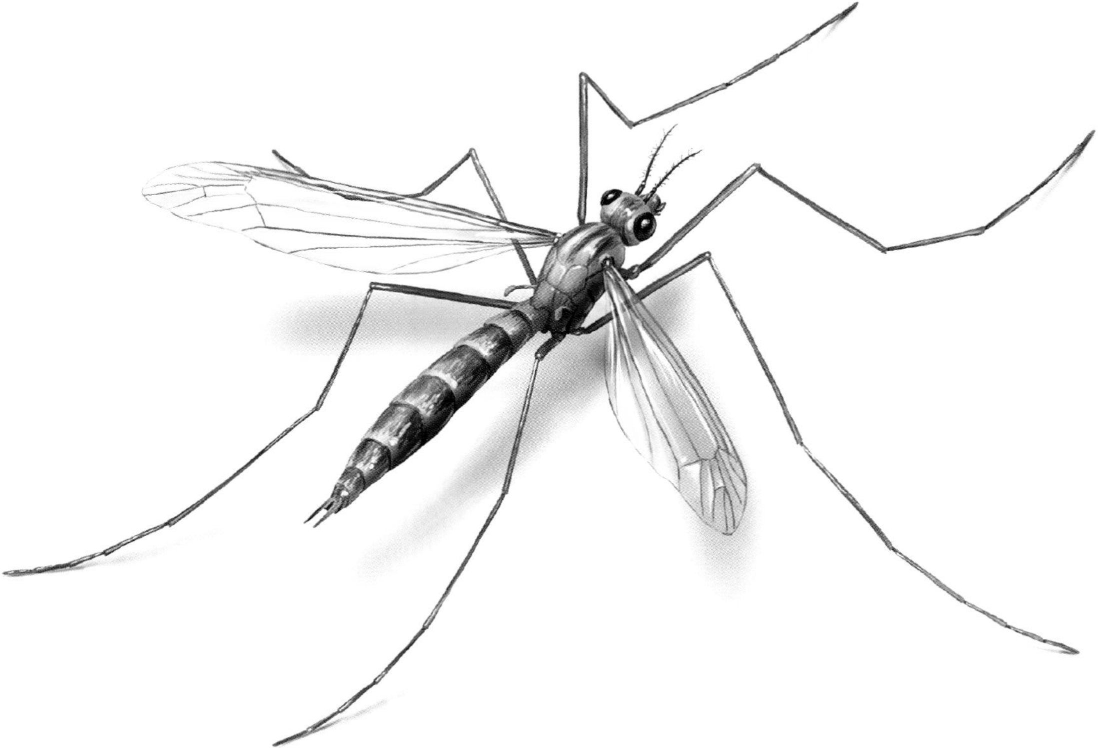

Missouri Bee Killer

SPECIES:
Proctacanthus milbertii

HABITAT AND FOOD:

LIFE CYCLE:

A species of robber fly, bee killers are nimble predators. They capture other flying insects in midair, then land and eat them. They have large, round eyes that help them find prey, and their long, tapered abdomens give them speed in flight. Missouri bee killers are known to eat honeybees.

Missouri bee killers can be found throughout the Midwest. They live in arid, sunny regions, such as open meadows and grasslands. Adults feed on other flying insects, but females will also feed on nectar sources to gather sugar for egg production. Larvae move around in decaying wood or in the ground, feeding on insect eggs or other soft-bodied insects.

Adult Missouri bee killers are common in the late summer months. Mated females lay eggs on low-lying plants or grasses. The eggs hatch and the larva fall to the ground, where they burrow under. They spend the winter as larvae and pupate in the spring. Just before emerging as adults, the pupae wriggle to the surface.

Drab coloring—browns, blacks and grays—hide bee killers from both predators and prey.

|0| | |1| | | |2| | |3| | |4| | |5| | |6|

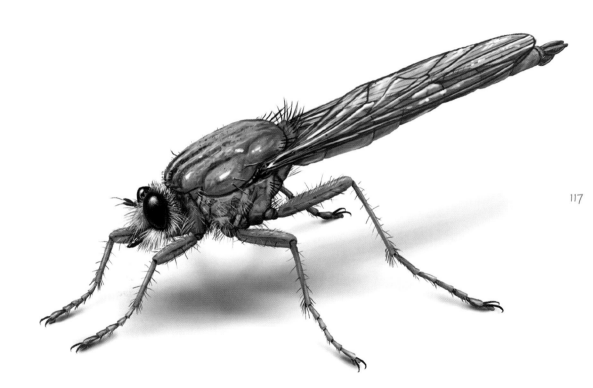

Scorpionfly

GENUS:
Panorpa

HABITAT AND FOOD:

LIFE CYCLE:

Scorpionflies are so-named because some of them have tails that look like scorpion stingers. Only males have these "stingers," which are actually organs used in mating. Scorpionflies are hard to see up close because they fly so quickly. You can find them on low plants along wooded trails, but you have to walk very slowly to avoid scaring them away.

Mostly found in the undergrowth of open woods and forest edges, scorpionfly larvae and adults eat dead insects. Scorpionflies as well as ants keep the forest floor clean of dead insects.

Scorpionfly larvae stay underground. They create burrows underneath dead insects. They overwinter as pupae and become adults in the spring. When courting, the male will present a female with a dead insect to persuade her to choose him. In the early summer, the females lay eggs in the soil, and they take about a week to hatch.

The long snout is designed to help the scorpionfly steal dead insects from spiders without getting trapped in their webs.

| 0 | | | | 1 | | | | 2 | | | | 3 | | | | 4 | | | | 5 | | | | 6 |

119

Glossary

Abdomen
The hind part of the insect or spider. This is where most of an insect's guts are found.

Arthropod
A phylum (large group) of animals that include the insects, spiders and centipedes as well as shrimps, crabs and fossil trilobites.

Caste
A special group of members in an ant or termite colony. Different groups of members look different and do different jobs to keep the colony healthy.

Cephalothorax
This is the front half of spiders. It includes the eyes and mouthparts as well as the legs.

Colony
A group of insects that live with their family members for protection and finding food.

Decomposer
An insect that eats dead things. Decomposers break down dead plants and animals in order to release their nutrients back to the soil.

Elytra

Elytra are beetles' hard forewings. Beetles don't use them for flying, only for protection.

Exoskeleton

A skeleton made of hard plates on the outside of an insect's body. Insects need them because their bodies don't have internal skeletons.

Genus

This is the first part of a creature's scientific name, which includes both genus and species (see the entry for "order"). Together, the genus and species names make up what scientists call "binomial nomenclature," or a "two-name" system of identifying plants and animals.

Habitat

The type of area where an insect gets its shelter, food and water. Different insects need different kinds of habitat.

Larva

A young insect that goes through complete metamorphosis. Beetles, flies and moths do this. (Young insects that go through incomplete metamorphosis are called nymphs.)

Metamorphosis

A growth process made up of separate life stages of development. There are two kinds of metamorphosis: incomplete and complete.

Molt

Molt is another word for shed. In order grow, insects shed their old, tight exoskeletons and rest briefly until the new skeletal plates harden over their soft, exposed bodies.

Nymph

A young insect that goes through incomplete metamorphosis. Dragonflies, grasshoppers and cockroaches do this. (Young insects that go through complete metamorphosis are called larvae.)

Order

A level of organization in the system that scientists use to classify living things. This system begins with the largest group at the top and ends with the smallest group at the bottom: kingdom, phylum, class, order, family, genus and species.

Palps

Little limbs on either side of a spider's mouth (right next to its fangs) that it uses to feel and hold food as it eats.

Pollination

The transfer of pollen from one flower to another, usually with the help of an insect. Without pollination, flowering plants will not produce fruit or seeds.

Predator

An insect or spider that eats other animals, usually other insects or spiders.

Pupa

The last stage a young insect goes through in the process of complete metamorphosis. "Pupation" often occurs in cocoons.

Subterranean

To live under ground.

Thorax

The middle section of the insect. This is where the wings and legs attach to the body.

Index

Species list by Order Grouping

Species by common name
(scientific name in parentheses)

For Further Reading

FREE PUBLICATIONS FROM MISSOURI DEPARTMENT OF CONSERVATION

Order the following FREE publications by e-mailing pubstaff@mdc.mo.gov or call (573) 522-4115, ext. 3630.

Butterfly Gardening and Conservation

Common Missouri Wasps and Bees

BOOKS AND DISKS FROM THE NATURE SHOP

Order the following publications online at mdcnatureshop.com or call 877-521-8632 (toll free) from 8 a.m. to 5 p.m. CST (central standard time), Monday through Friday except holidays.

Native Landscaping for Wildlife and People by Dave Tylka, Missouri Department of Conservation 2002

Butterflies and Moths of Missouri by J. Richard and Joan E. Heitzman, Missouri Department of Conservation 1996

Singing Insects of Missouri cassette or CD, both with poster

FIELD GUIDES AND OTHER BOOKS

Peterson First Guides

Caterpillars by Amy Bartlett Wright and Roger Tory Peterson, 1998

Butterflies and Moths by Paul A. Opler, et al., 1998

Insects of North America by Christopher Leahy, 1998

Dover Little Activity Books
> Learning about Insects by Jan Sovak
>
> Learning about Spiders by Jan Sovak
>
> Little Insects Coloring Book by Winky Adam

DVDs

Eyewitness Video Series: Insects
narrated by Martin Sheen 1994

Web Sites

www.bugsurvey.nsw.gov.au/

www.insects.org/index.html

www.whatsthiscaterpillar.co.uk/america/index.htm

www.xerces.org

129

$\mathcal{C}$urrently pursuing his doctorate in entomology at Michigan State University, Mike received his master's degree in entomology from the University of Missouri in 2006. A former entomology research assistant for the United States Department of Agriculture, Mike enjoys roaming the countryside collecting and studying insects, especially beetles and aphids.

A conservatory-trained pianist, Steve Buchanan left his post as a college music professor to become a nature artist. Painting with his computer, he has created art for books, magazines, T-shirts, posters, product labels and United States postage stamps. He especially likes to paint bugs that appear to be made of metallic foil.

Acknowledgments

The production team would like to thank several Missouri Department of Conservation staff members for their help with this book. St. Louis Region Natural History Biologist Mike Arduser, former Runge Nature Center Naturalist Andrea Putnam and Resource Scientist Rob Lawrence helped us decide which 50 species of arthropods to feature. Rob continued to advise us about species details and illustrations. Wildlife Programs Supervisor Dennis Figg put his training and experience as an entomologist to work for us as he reviewed the text and layout, helping us make sure our presentation is as clear and accurate as possible. *We thank you all!*